SMART SHOPPING

CLEARANCE

50%OFF

regular or original price as ticketed

intermediate markdowns may have been taken prior to being designated as clearance

L   M   S

Peachtree

CECILIA MINDEN

Published in the United States of America by Cherry Lake Publishing
Ann Arbor, Michigan
www.cherrylakepublishing.com

Math Education: Dr. Timothy Whiteford, Associate Professor of Education at St. Michael's College
Financial Adviser: Kenneth Klooster, financial adviser at Edward Jones Investments
Reading Adviser: Marla Conn, ReadAbility, Inc.

Photo Credits: © Arina P Habich/Shutterstock Images, cover, 1; © Rob Marmion/Shutterstock Images, 5; © nito/
Shutterstock Images, 7; © Monkey Business Images/Shutterstock Images, 9; © digitalskillet/Thinkstock.com, 10; ©
Costinescu | Dreamstime.com - Shopping List Photo, 13; © Denys Prykhodov/Shutterstock Images, 15; © Kim Reinick/
Shutterstock Images, 17; © Zurijeta/Shutterstock Images, 19; © Juanmonino/iStock.com, 21; © Lisa F. Young/
Shutterstock Images, 22; © Digital Vision/Thinkstock.com, 25; © VikramRaghuvanshi/iStock.com, 27; © Goodluz/
Shutterstock Images, 29

Library of Congress Cataloging-in-Publication Data

Minden, Cecilia.
      Smart shopping / Cecilia Minden.
   pages cm. — (Real world math: personal finance)
   Includes bibliographical references and index.
   ISBN 978-1-63362-575-4 (hardcover) — ISBN 978-1-63362-755-0 (pdf) — ISBN 978-1-63362-665-2 (pbk.) —
   ISBN 978-1-63362-845-8 (ebook) 1. Shopping—Mathematics—Juvenile literature. 2. Consumer education—Juvenile
   literature. 3. Finance, Personal—Juvenile literature. 4. Mathematics—Juvenile literature. I. Title.

   TX335.5.M56 2016
   381'.10151—dc23   2015008972

Cherry Lake Publishing would like to acknowledge the work of
the Partnership for 21st Century Skills. Please visit www.p21.org
for more information.

Printed in the United States of America
Corporate Graphics

ABOUT THE AUTHOR

Cecilia Minden, PhD, is a literacy consultant and the author of many books for children. She is the former director of the Language and Literacy Program at the Harvard Graduate School of Education in Cambridge, Massachusetts. Dr. Minden enjoys shopping, especially sales with discount coupons!

TABLE OF CONTENTS

THE TWEEN CONSUMER

If you are a tween—meaning you are between the ages of 10 and 13—then you are among the top **consumers** in the United States. Consumers are people who pay for goods and services. Since most tweens do not need to pay for food, clothing, and rent, and often get allowances for doing chores, they have **disposable income**. This means they have many choices on how to spend their money.

Tweens often want to buy different things than adults do.

Shopping is fun for some people and a chore for others. For all of us, though, it is the way we get what we want and need. Where do you shop? Do you shop at stores in the mall or downtown? Do you shop at thrift stores, yard sales, or farmers' markets? Do you shop online?

With so many choices, how can you become a smart shopper? How do you decide where and what to buy? How can you get the best prices? Let's find out!

21ST CENTURY CONTENT

Today, many consumers shop on the Internet. Thousands of Web sites provide consumers with choices from around the world. You can shop for masks from Africa, sweaters from Ireland, or guitars from Brazil without ever leaving your home. The Internet makes it easy to access goods from all over the world and have the products delivered to your home.

Don't ignore yard sales and flea markets. One person's trash is another person's treasure!

CHAPTER 2

I WANT/NEED THAT!

Needing something means you have to have it to survive. We need to wear clothing to protect us from the weather. If that's all there were to it, we could all wear the same clothes. Boring! We are all individuals with different body types and tastes. While we may all need clothing, we want to make different choices in the clothing we buy. You may prefer to have something that's a certain color, or a certain brand, even when a different option might be much cheaper.

Checking prices online can save you time and money.

A winter coat is something you'll wear pretty often, so be sure to make the right choice.

For example, you need a new winter coat. Your old coat has holes in it and is too small. It will not keep you warm. Many of your friends are wearing a certain brand of coat, but it costs more than your parents want to spend. How can you decide if that expensive coat is a want or a need?

Consider different points of view before you choose what to buy. You really, really want that expensive coat—but how practical is it? Does it have enough pockets for what you carry around? Is it appropriate for the weather where you live? Will it match with most of your other clothes? You should also like the way it looks on you. Take a picture of yourself wearing it and send it to your friends. Do they think it's worth the money?

Shop around. Check the price of this coat at several stores and keep track of those numbers. Try looking online also. Look at all the possibilities before making a final decision. If you still can't make up your mind, ask the store to hold the coat for you for a day while you think it over.

LIFE AND CAREER SKILLS

Deciding between what you want and what you need can be a great way to exercise **reasoning** skills and learn how to make choices. You will get pressure from ads in magazines and on TV, your computer, and billboards. Ads use special photography, music, and celebrities to promote their products. Don't be swayed. Make up your own mind about what you want to buy.

Always make a list when you go shopping. What do you need to buy now? Are there things on the list that would be nice to have but are not needed? Do you have any coupons? Where are the sales? Include a cost estimate for each item. Do some online research at stores' Web sites to get a realistic idea of prices and quality. Comparing prices ahead of time saves time and money.

REAL WORLD MATH CHALLENGE

Nick saved up $25.00 for a new basketball. Super Sports has the one he wants for $28.00. Drew Athletics sells the same basketball for $30.00, but it is on sale for 15 percent off through the end of the month. Sales tax is 5 percent.

- Which store has the lower price?
- How much more money does Nick need to buy the basketball at the store with the lower price?

(Turn to page 30 for the answers)

Before you shop, try to plan what you need.

Do the Math: Getting the Best Price

You know what you want and how much money you can spend. How can you get the best price for what you want to buy? One way is to buy off-season. Winter clothing often goes on sale in February, and July is a good time to find bargains on summer clothes. Stores need to make room for newer seasonal **merchandise**. The end of every season is a good time to search stores for items to use the following year. Search your local newspaper for coupons and advertisements.

Discount stores buy merchandise in large quantities

Buying summer clothes in the winter is one way to get a good deal.

and offer them at lower prices. This is a good place to stock up on items that you know you will need and use, if the brand doesn't matter. If an item isn't on the shelf, ask a salesperson if there might be another one in the storeroom. There are Web sites designed to help you save money by offering discounts and coupons. Be sure to ask an adult before ordering from them.

Outlet stores sell name brands at reduced costs. Merchandise is frequently off-season or slightly damaged. With a little effort, you can get popular brands at bargain prices. Don't be afraid to ask for an additional discount if something is torn or stained. A little skill with a needle or a bottle of stain remover will make it good as new.

Coupons are a great way to save. Invented in 1895, they were first used to promote a new soft drink, Coca-Cola. More than 100 years later, The Coca-Cola Company is still offering coupons to sell its products! It is important to read coupons carefully. Sometimes **restrictions** may apply. Smart shoppers do their math to decide if a discount at one store or a coupon at another will give them the best price.

Life and Career Skills

Take advantage of discount prices at movies by going in the afternoon. Admission is cheaper, and some theaters even offer cheaper popcorn and soft drinks in the afternoon.

Look for coupons in newspapers and online. Be sure to check when the coupons expire.

REAL WORLD MATH CHALLENGE

Paige is shopping for a new sweater. She has $30.00 to spend. She found a newspaper coupon for 20 percent off one item at Lynn's Garment Garden. The coupon can't be used for sale items. At the store, Paige found a pretty purple sweater for $34.95. It is not on sale. She also found a pretty pink sweater on sale for $28.95.

- Which sweater will cost less?
- How much less?

(Turn to page 30 for the answers)

CHAPTER 4

Do the Math: Consider Other Costs

You found what you were looking for at a great price. What other costs should you consider? Nearly all states charge a sales tax, but these taxes differ from state to state. Massachusetts, for example, doesn't charge sales tax on clothing but does charge sales tax on other items. The amount of tax charged will also depend on what you buy. You may pay a higher tax on luxury items such as televisions or expensive clothing. Necessities such as food or medical items may have a lower tax or none at all.

Always allow for sales tax when figuring the final cost of your purchase.

REAL WORLD MATH CHALLENGE

Sales tax is a percentage of the basic price of an item. For example, Kyle goes to the grocery store to buy snacks for his soccer team. His purchase comes to $23.46 before tax. State and local taxes total 7 percent. Kyle has $25.00 to spend.

- Does he have enough money to pay for his purchase? Add the purchase price and taxes to find out what the item really costs.

(Turn to page 30 for the answers)

A quick way to add up costs is to round up to an even number. This will give you an estimate before you get to the checkout counter. For example, you have three items for $4.62, $3.75, and $2.64. By rounding up, you can quickly add 5 + 4 + 3 = 12. Add a few cents for sales tax and you will know if you have enough money to pay for everything.

If you are buying items from another city or state, you will usually have to pay for the store to ship it to you. Shipping costs depend on where the item is located and

Using a calculator can help you find the best deals.

When you shop online, you'll usually need to pay for shipping.

where and how you want it shipped. Other factors include package weight and how quickly you want to receive the item. Sometimes there are special handling costs such as extra packing for items that might break. Stores frequently offer special deals giving you free shipping if your items cost more than a certain amount. Get together with family and friends to make one big order and avoid shipping costs.

REAL WORLD MATH CHALLENGE

Accidents can cause unexpected expenses. Mateo and Mia accidentally broke Mom's favorite vase. They searched online and found one just like it for $15.00. Tax is 7 percent, and shipping costs are $2.99 plus $0.59 per pound. The vase weighs 2 pounds. They tell their mom they will give her the money to order the vase online.

- How much money do Mateo and Mia need to replace the broken vase?
- If Mateo and Mia agree to split the cost evenly, how much do they each have to contribute toward the cost of the vase?

(Turn to page 30 for the answers)

How to Be a Smarter Shopper

You've made a list, compared prices, gathered coupons, and set aside extra cash for taxes. A few more tips will help make your shopping trip the best ever.

Since you'll probably do most of your shopping on weekends or holidays, get an early start to avoid long lines. Be sure to carry money in a secure pocket or purse, and always wear comfortable shoes! Are you going to a familiar mall? Plan which stores to visit according to your shopping lists.

Shopping with good friends can be a lot of fun.

LIFE AND CAREER SKILLS

Shopping with a group of family members or friends can be a test of your problem-solving skills and flexibility. You will need to work together to come up with a plan that lets everyone shop for what he or she wants. Decide on a place to meet if you get separated. Choose a time to meet for the trip home. Being flexible and making sure everyone has a good time can make the shopping trip fun for everyone.

Maybe you prefer to shop online. The Internet is convenient, and you can find some great deals. But there are guidelines to follow to make a safe purchase. You need to compare and consider Web offers just as you would in any store.

A general rule to follow is that if something sounds too good to be true, then it probably is. Check a Web site thoroughly and get an adult's permission before entering any personal information, especially information that gives the Web site access to a bank account or credit card. You should never have to reveal

Only shop on Web sites you trust. If you aren't
sure about one, read reviews of it on other sites.

Always check with a parent before buying anything online.

your Social Security number. If you do get adult
permission to make a purchase, look for a padlock **icon**
on your screen. That is one way to tell you are on a
secure site. Another way to tell is if the letters "http" in
the **URL** change to "https." The "s" means "secure."
Remember, to help you avoid an online shopping disaster,
always check with an adult before making a purchase.

Smart shopping is fun. It is like a game or mystery.
You put together all the clues and figure out the best
way to solve the puzzle. Saving money means you can

either buy more or put the money you save aside for another day. Smart shoppers enjoy new purchases because they know that they put in the time and effort necessary to get what they really wanted at a price they could afford. Let's go shopping!

REAL WORLD MATH CHALLENGE

Patrick received $45.00 for his birthday. He earned $60.00 mowing lawns. He wants to buy a rack to hold all of his DVDs, but he also wants to buy a new speaker and a computer game. He searched several places online and found that Grandpa's Store has the best prices for all those products. Another store, Kelly's Computers, won't charge for shipping if his order total is more than $90.00. The rack at Grandpa's Store costs $31.99 and will hold 150 DVDs. The shipping cost is $10.00. Kelly's Computers has a better-quality rack for $45.95 that also holds 150 DVDs. He has a coupon for 15 percent off one item at Kelly's Computers. At both places, the speaker is $35.95, and the computer game is $29.95. There is a 5 percent sales tax on the total.

- Try making an organized list of the prices. What would Patrick's total cost be at Grandpa's Store if he buys the DVD rack, the speaker, and the game?
- At Kelly's Computers?
- Does Patrick have enough money for everything?

(Turn to page 30 for the answers)

REAL WORLD MATH CHALLENGE ANSWERS

CHAPTER TWO
Page 12
The basketball at Drew Athletics is $25.50 before tax.
Drew Athletics has the lower price.
$30.00 for the basketball x 0.15 discount = $4.50
$30.00 − $4.50 = $25.50 is the discounted price of the basketball
$25.50 x 0.05 sales tax = $1.28 (rounded up from $1.275)
$25.50 + $1.28 = $26.78 for the basketball

Nick only has $25.00.
$26.78 − $25.00 = $1.78
Nick needs $1.78 more to be able to purchase the basketball.

CHAPTER THREE
Page 17
The purple sweater will cost less.
$34.95 for the purple sweater x 0.20 discount = $6.99
$34.95 − $6.99 = $27.96 for the purple sweater

The purple sweater costs $0.99 less than the pink sweater.
$28.95 for the pink sweater − $27.96 = $0.99

CHAPTER FOUR
Page 20
Kyle does not have enough money to pay for his purchase. He is short by $0.10.
$23.46 for the snacks x 0.07 sales tax = $1.64
$23.46 + $1.64 = $25.10 total for the snacks
$25.10 − $25.00 = $0.10

Page 23
Mateo and Mia need $20.22 to replace the vase.
$15.00 for the vase x 0.07 sales tax = $1.05 tax
2 pounds x $0.59 per pound = $1.18 for part of the shipping cost
$2.99 + $1.18 = $4.17 total shipping cost
$15.00 + $1.05 + $4.17 = $20.22

Mateo and Mia each need to give Mom $10.11.
$20.22 ÷ 2 = $10.11

CHAPTER FIVE
Page 29
The total cost at Grandpa's Store would be $112.78.
$31.99 for the rack + $35.95 for the speaker + $29.95 for the computer game = $97.89
$97.89 x 0.05 tax = $4.89
$97.89 + $4.89 + $10 shipping = $112.78

The total cost at Kelly's Computers would be $110.21.
$45.95 for the rack x 0.15 discount = $6.89
$45.95 − $6.89 = $39.06 for the rack
$39.06 + $35.95 for the speaker + $29.95 for the computer game = $104.96
$104.96 x 0.05 tax = $5.25
$104.96 + $5.25 + 0 for shipping = $110.21

Patrick does not have enough money to buy everything. If he buys all three items at Kelly's Computers, which costs less than Grandpa's, he will still need $5.21.
$45.00 for his birthday + $60.00 for mowing lawns = $105.00
$110.21 - $105.00 = $5.21

FIND OUT MORE

BOOKS

Einspruch, Andrew. *Smart Shopping*. Mankato, MN: Smart Apple Media, 2011.

Peterson, Judy Monroe. *Digital Smarts: How to Stay Within a Budget When Shopping, Living, and Doing Business Online*. New York: Rosen Publishing, 2012.

WEB SITES

FTC—You Are Here: Where Kids Learn to Be Smarter Consumers
www.consumer.ftc.gov/sites/default/files/games/off-site/youarehere/index.html
A virtual mall with games and activities to help you be a better consumer.

PBS Kids—Don't Buy It: Get Media Smart
http://pbskids.org/dontbuyit/buyingsmart/
Get ideas and questions to consider when shopping.

GLOSSARY

consumers (kuhn-SOO-murz) people who buy goods and services

disposable income (dis-POH-zuh-buhl IN-kuhm) money available to be spent or saved as one wishes

icon (EYE-kahn) a picture that represents something

merchandise (MUR-chuhn-dise) goods that are bought or sold

reasoning (REE-zuh-ning) the process of thinking in an orderly fashion, drawing conclusions from facts

restrictions (rih-STRIK-shuhnz) limitations on the use of something

URL (YU-AR-EL) the address of a Web site on the Internet; stands for uniform resource locator or universal resource locator

INDEX

[21ST CENTURY SKILLS LIBRARY]

Peachtree

Atlanta-Fulton Public Library